With love, to EARTH'S ENDANGERED PEOPLES

BY
VIRGINIA KROLL

ILLUSTRATED BY
ROBERTA COLLIER-MORALES

This book is dedicated, with love, to all Earth's children with special thoughts to Mandy, Jessica, Kimberly, and Rebecca, my nieces, and Jeremy, Michael, and Gregory, my nephews. —VK

This work is dedicated to God, to aboriginal people all over the planet, and to my parents and family—who seem always to love me, even after a long day's work when I appear with hair disheveled, chalk on my face, and not a clue what to make for dinner! —RC-M

Library of Congress Cataloging-in-Publication Data

Kroll, Virginia L.
    With love, to earth's endangered people / by Virginia Kroll ; illustrated by Roberta Collier-Morales. – 1ˢᵗ ed.
        p. cm.
        SUMMARY: an introduction to the endangered cultures of the Quechua, Ainu, Bushmen, Toda, Inuit, Mbuti, and Aborigine.
        ISBN: 1-883220-83-1 (case)
        ISBN: 1-883220-82-3 (pbk.)

    1. Indigenous peoples—Juvenile literature. 2. Ethnology—Juvenile literature. I. Collier-Morales, Roberta, ill. II. Title.

GN380.K76 1998   306'.08
                                              QBI98-690

Dawn Publications
14618 Tyler Foote Road
Nevada City, CA 95959
800-545-7475
Email: DawnPub@oro.net
Website: www.DawnPub.com

Printed in China

10 9 8 7 6 5 4 3 2 1
First Edition

Cover and interior design by Renee Glenn Designs
Other computer production by Rob Froelick

Dear children everywhere,

All over the world, groups of people, like species of animals, are endangered. Like the Native Americans of North America, their age-old ways of living are in danger of being lost forever. Often these people have a beautiful, meaningful relationship with the Earth, and with each other. This book portrays some of them, with love.

Sincerely,

Virginia Kroll

DEAR QUECHUA CHILDREN,

Your woven clothing
brightens the stony slopes
as you graze the llamas
that bear your burdens.

✳

Your hearts soar at the sight of condors
aloft on the Andean air
and thrill at the tweaks and squeaks
of shy, hiding cavies
as they skitter in the scrub.

Condors, magnificent birds of prey, live near the Quechua people of South America's Andes Mountains, as do **cavies**, wild rodents from which guinea pigs are descended. The Quechua herd **llamas**, beasts of burden related to camels, and use their wool to make multi-colored hats, shawls, clothing and blankets. They farm on small patches of land, growing crops which include corn, potatoes, beans, grapes and quinoa, a plant whose seeds are ground and used as cereal.

Your older brothers' flutes
echo off rain-stirred streams
and trill though the valley
as they talk to God
through the music of your Inca ancestors.

＊

Your grandparents
look into people's hearts
and heal their hurts
with natural knowledge.

The music of the Quechua, whose
ancestors were Incas, is beautiful, haunting and full of prayer.
The older people of the tribe
who are healers, or **shamans**,
know which plants and other
substances from nature ease
pain and cure many sicknesses.

Who will lead the llamas?

✳

Who will remind others,
your sisters and brothers,
that we are **all** part of nature
if you leave the mountaintop,
colorful Quechua?

DEAR AINU CHILDREN,

Your parents rock you in shintas
suspended from your ceilings,
and sing you lullabies about
beloved bear.

The sacred prayer stick,
made by your uncles of peeled willow stem,
blesses the fire pit
where crab and flounder,
squid and salmon sizzle.

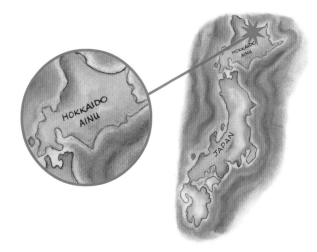

Living on Japan's northernmost island, Hokkaido, the Ainu live through bitter winters. Unlike other Japanese, their eyes are rounded and their hair is wavy. Ainu women used to tattoo around their mouths with birchbark soot. This was considered a mark of beauty and status. They bless their cooking fires with specially carved prayer sticks call **inau**. **Shintas** are hanging cradles for babies.

Your aunts and mothers gather kelp,
another of Ocean's gifts,
to make into soups, relishes, and iodine
for the bitter, biting winter.

✳

In summer, you shade your round eyes
and wavy hair
with large leaves of the butterbur tree,
turned into umbrellas.
You learn to embroider life into your fabrics
with every stitch and loop and knot
of your ikarakara.

The Ainu believe that their detailed, skillful embroidery, called **ikarakara**, turns sewn designs into living beings. In their religion, "spirit beings" called kamui live in their own world, but sometimes visit their villages as animals. Legend says that once a giant bear came from the sky to save the people from a great famine. They revere the bear, and much of their folklore includes him.

Who will call upon the kamui,
the spirits of fire, sea, air and animals?

✳

Who will ever be as peaceful and gentle,
yet as fierce and courageous all at once,
if you meld into the mainland,
admirable Ainu?

Ainu people eat ocean plants
and seafood, sometimes
hunting fish with bow and
arrow, and play a
twanging stringed
instrument, called a
mukkuri, made of
bamboo.

DEAR BUSHMAN CHILDREN,

Your mamas cuddle you
and string eggshell beads
around your necks
to keep harm and danger away.
Your cousins use stones
as hones to sharpen knives.

You collect the eggs of ostriches
to use as canteens.
Your fathers fashion leather
armlets for your mothers
from the scraps of hides
they have hunted.

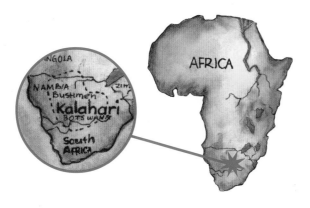

Bushmen people wander the Kalahari Desert in southern Africa, where temperatures are extremely hot by day and extremely cold by night. They possess an amazing ability to find water, storing it in ostrich eggshells, which they sometimes decorate. They also break the eggshells to make tiny beads, which they string into necklaces for their babies, to ward off evil.

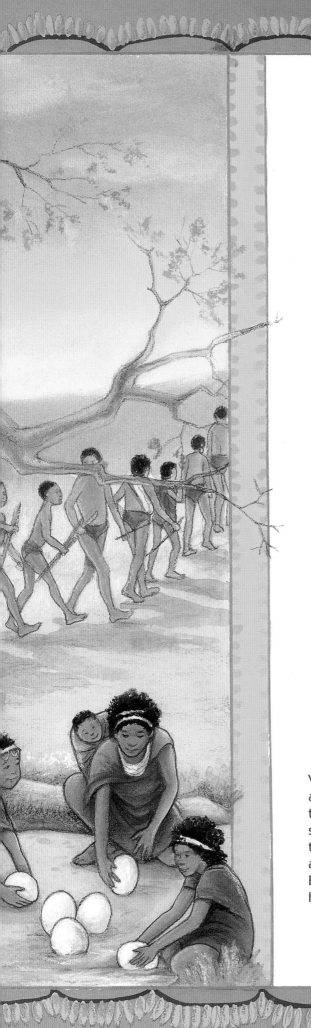

The females in your family
forage daily for food
and carry it home in kaross capes.
Lizards look from shady hideaways
and meerkats marvel as you migrate—
barefoot—over the searing sand.

✳

Later you stop to play tossing games,
using melons as balls.

While men hunt large animals such as the **eland antelope** as well as snakes and lizards for food, women go off together, often having to travel very far, to gather nuts, shiny round melons, roots and berries. A woman wraps these foods in a **kaross**, a cape made from the skin of antelopes. A kaross is used as a baby-tote as well. In Bushmen society, everything is shared. No one goes hungry, thirsty or without shelter.

Who will warm the desert at dawn
with crackling campfires?

*

Who will know just where the
roots and melons are
if no more of you roam the Kalahari,
beautiful Bushman?

Their primary musical instrument is a chain of ankle rattles, cocoons filled with ostrich eggshell bits. They also play a five-stringed instrument, a **guashi**, to express joy or sorrow. Many types of lizards inhabit the Kalahari, and **meerkats**, a type of mongoose, live in colonies.

DEAR TODA CHILDREN,

Your people are elegant
in their cloaks of red and black and white.
The long, tight curls of your mothers
are astir in the chilly breeze
of your hilly home.

In the pasture, you pat your buffalo,
getting to know each animal well
by its name and nature.

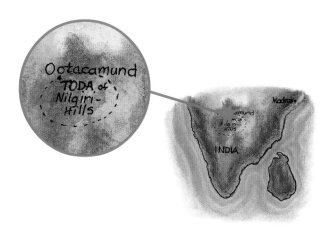

The Toda live in the Nilgiri Hills of southern India. Both men and women wear **putkulis**, one-piece white cotton cloaks that are decorated with red and black embroidery. All aspects of Toda life revolve around the sacred buffalo.

Your men are in the temple,
praying, fasting and thatching the roof.
When the temple is completed,
your men hold hands
and dance in celebration,
looking to the sun to gain strength and luck
for coping with life's pain.

Each of you knows your very own role;
community spirit binds you
like vines entwined.
When one man sins, all of you suffer.
When one woman revels,
the rest of you rejoice.

Men mend the temples and practice the religious
rituals. Priests, who alone live in the temples, churn the
buffalos' milk to make a special butter called ghee.
Each priest carries with him a bamboo milk container
and a churn.

The remarkable Toda spirit of community and oneness
insures that each individual has his or her own specific
jobs to do and particular place in society. Each member
of the group feels deeply responsible for the welfare of
everyone else.

W ho will stir the butter
in its bamboo churn?

*

W ho will revere the buffalo
and light the temple lamps
if your old ways are abandoned,
talented Toda?

The Toda have several rituals involving the sun.
One involves publicly introducing a three-month-old
baby to the community by showing its face at daybreak
after the first bird sings.

DEAR INUIT CHILDREN,

Your beloved elders' fine-lined faces
crinkle in the cold
where everything crackles
in The Beautiful Land.

They tell of white-coated creatures
running from raw, clawing wind
to nestle in drafty niches and dreamy nooks.
They thank Whale and Seal,
Goose and Caribou,
Murre and Musk Ox, Walrus and Wolverine,
Fish and Fox for blessing your people
with oil, blubber, bone, food, and fur.

The Inuit, from the tundra regions of northern Alaska,
northern Canada, northern Russia and Greenland, are
among the most resourceful of Earth's peoples. Until
recently, they fashioned everything they needed from
the natural resources found in their frigid, frozen
surroundings. They call their land "Beautiful."

Your grandfathers' ivory fishhooks,
harpoon heads, spirit masks
and soapstone sculptures are works of art.

✳

Your driftwood dogsleds speed you
through the snow,
and you are already learning
that life's secret is found in
flowing with Nature,
not in fighting against her.

They appreciate their fellow creatures that give their
lives so that the Inuit people can be warm and well-
fed. Customs, such as giving a slain animal a drink of
sparkling water to send its spirit properly out of its
body, are important parts of the Inuit hunt. Wooden
masks were worn by angakoks, men and women with
special powers, during ceremonies to honor the spirits.

W ho will send speared seals
to the spirit world
with whispered words
and sips of glistening water?

✳

W ho will thank your
brother and sister creatures
for giving their lives
if you change your cherished customs,
ingenious Inuit?

Even today, when guns are used instead of harpoons
and snowmobiles driven in place of dogsleds, the
Inuit have not lost touch with the belief that nature is
to be heeded, respected, protected and cherished.

Dear Mbuti Children,

You wear only bits of bark, fallen feathers
and strings of beads made of nuts and seeds.
You call your forest "Mother"
and sing her poems of praise.

You bathe in daily rain showers
and sleep in sound, round huts,
your bodies covered with bark cloth blankets
that your parents have borrowed, gently,
from the fig tree's inner layer.

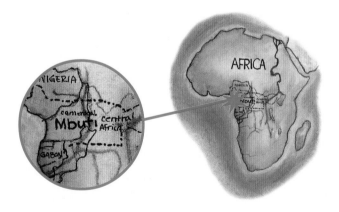

The Mbuti people of central Africa's Ituri forest call
their rainforest "Mother." They wake her each morning
and ask for protection. They make bark cloth blankets
(and aprons, which are sometimes worn by adults)
from the inner bark of the fig tree, which they strip
very carefully so as not to damage the tree. The layer
is soaked, then pounded into softness with an
elephant tusk tool.

Your papas stare down the leopard
and let him live,
for you do not need his flesh to feed you
or his hide to clothe you.

✳

Instead, your grandmothers gather bulbs
in "burden baskets,"
and no one ever wastes a shoot or root
or ounce of antelope meat
that your older brothers have captured
and brought back to camp for one and all.

They hunt the small forest-dwelling **duiker antelope**.
Nothing is wasted, for the Mbuti believe in taking only
what is needed. As with Bushmen and Aborigines, all
is shared, and no one is needy among the tribe. Until
recently, outsiders feared the spirits believed to dwell
in the forest and allowed the Mbuti to give them
treasures of the forest gradually. Now, however, the
habitat is greatly endangered because it is being
destroyed by outsiders with no consideration for the
balance of nature.

W ho will dance to celebrate
Mother Forest?

✳

Who will stop the thundering
of falling leafy giants
if others take over your hidden hollow,
marvelous Mbuti?

The Mbuti are rich in storytelling and poetry. Often
they compose songs with beautiful lyrics to accom-
pany their dances, which are joyful responses to the
bounty and blessings given by the Creator, who has
made Mother Forest for them.

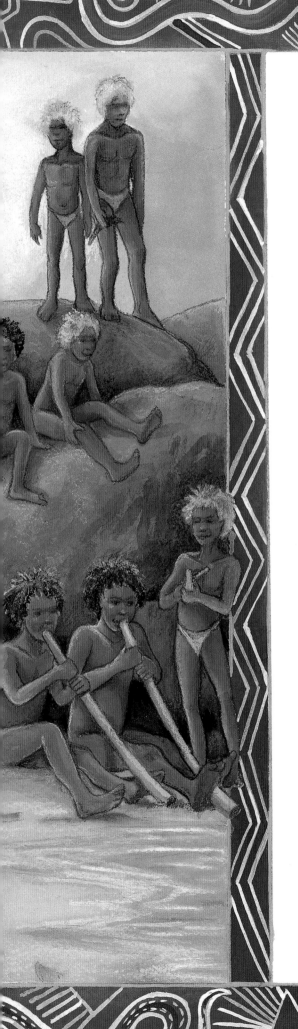

DEAR ABORIGINE CHILDREN,

You tiptoe barefoot on boulders,
your hair kissed golden
by Australia's gleaming sun.
Tracks of kangaroos and emus, too,
blend with yours on the sparkling shore.

✳

Your brothers' digeridoos haunt the land
with sounds that mimic trickling tidepools
and rumbling thunder.
Your language holds no word for "hate."
To your folks, that is an unknown feeling.

AUSTRALIA
Aborigine

Young Aborigines have blond hair. Music is made by
playing the **digeridoo**, an instrument made from a
hollow tree limb, or by clapping sticks or **boomerangs**
together. Love, harmony and calmness characterize
the disposition of the people, and selfishness is
unheard of in their culture.

You wonder at wombat
and laugh with kookaburra
while bell birds tinkle their greetings
from silver gum trees.

✳

Your parents perfume the night
with sweet smoke of sandalwood fires.
The air bursts with the bangs of boomerangs
and clacks of clapping sticks
as they dance until dawn
with leaves tied onto muscled legs,
with smiles lighting glowing faces,
as you and your cousins doze.

They live among marsupials
(pouched mammals) such as
kangaroos, **wallaroos**, and **wombats**. Birds
in their midst include the large, flightless **emu**
(related to the ostrich), the "laugh-
ing" **kookaburra** (a type of king-
fisher), and smaller, melodious bell
birds. Sometimes they hunt by using boomerangs, curved imple-
ments that are thrown.

Who will see that no man marks
or harms the places
where your Creation Ancestors
are alive in everything?

✳

Who will keep
the dreaming places peaceful
if others push you off your ancient land,
amazing Aborigines?

To the Aborigines, the land was formed by Creation
Beings, who now live in everything from woods to water-
falls, just as the Aborigines will do when their bodies die.
Therefore, the land and these "dreaming places" must
never, ever be marked or harmed in any way.

A NOTE FROM THE AUTHOR ABOUT ENDANGERED PEOPLES, AND YOU

There are different reasons why groups of people become endangered.

- Sometimes foreigners enter a region carrying a disease that the bodies of people who have been isolated for centuries cannot fight. Whole villages can be wiped out from illness.

- Sometimes "modern" people make life hard for old-fashioned folks. Their land is sometimes taken by others for commercial use. Rainforests, for example, are wanted for logging and farming.

- Sometimes old ways die out with old people as their young people are lured into more modern ways.

Either by choice or by force, people may abandon their tribes and traditions. They become **assimilated**, or blended into, the main societies around them. Many cannot adapt to new ways and are rapidly disappearing. These peoples, who are so beautifully attuned to nature and its preservation, are leaving the Earth after being here for thousands of years.

The population of the peoples mentioned in my book have dwindled drastically in recent years for all these reasons.

- Approximately 45 percent of Peru's population is made up of Indians, including the **Quechua**. However, many have adopted western ways, begun to speak Spanish rather than their native languages, and have mixed with surrounding society. Therefore, it is impossible to ascertain exact population statistics.

- **Ainu**, the first people to live in Japan, number fewer than 16,000. Most live on the northern island of Hokkaido. Old ways, for most, are a thing of the past.

- **Bushmen** are being pushed deeper and deeper into the desert and are trying to deal with diminishing resources. Birth rates drop as people's food supplies shrink. Only 18,000 Bushmen still cling to their hunting and gathering lifestyle.

- Only 760 **Toda** descendants remain in southern India today, clinging to the old methods.

- Only 100,000 **Inuit** people inhabit Russia, Canada, Greenland and Alaska. Most have adopted modern ways.

- There are fewer than 50,000 **Mbuti** people in Africa today, and many of them are mixed with other peoples. They cannot sustain their way of life without their Forest.

- Of the 206,000 **Aborigines** left in Australia today, only one-third are of unmixed descent. Many have moved into cities and are struggling to cope with modern life in populated areas.

Some other endangered people include the **Kraho**, **Waura**, and **Yanomami** of South America's Amazon River areas; the **Sarawak** and **Penan** peoples of Malaysia; the **Maori** of New Zealand; the **Lua** and **Hmong** of Thailand; the **Karir** of western Pakistan; and the **Chamula** of southern Mexico. **Lapps**, reindeer herders of Scandinavia, and cattle-loving **Masai** of East Africa share the same plight.

You may feel overwhelmed and hopeless at the idea of endangered people, but you have the power to do many positive things right where you are. Help each other in little ways. For example, you don't have to agree with a person or even like him or her, but respect toward everyone is basic. Explore the cultures of other people. Ask questions about a "different" holiday. Taste a "foreign" food. Emphasize the similarities that connect all people on this good Earth. All this can be done at home or in the classroom. Brotherly/sisterly love is sown in familiar gardens and flourishes, branching out from there.

I call upon all children to celebrate each other and to know, as they read this book, that no matter how our differences seem to make us unalike, we are all, undeniably, linked to one another. As Nobel Prize winner Bishop Desmond Tutu of South Africa has pointed out,

"…my humanity is bound up in yours, for we can only be human together."

VIRGINIA KROLL has had 37 children's books published since 1992. She has won several awards and has contributed over 1500 items to juvenile magazines. Her interest in Earth and nature began as a young child when she began to study the birds and wildlife in her own backyard. She is married to David Haeick and has three sons, three daughters, a granddaughter, and many pets. Virginia lives near Buffalo, New York. Her book *Motherlove* is also published by Dawn Publications.

As a child in school, **ROBERTA COLLIER-MORALES** peered out the window at the trees and mountains, and filled the margins of her papers—even her tests—with pictures. When her teachers moved her away from the window, she learned to draw from her imagination. She graduated with a degree in illustration from Colorado State University, then taught art in both Colorado and New York City. Now a professional illustrator, she lives with her two children and an extended family in Colorado.

NOW AVAILABLE

A Teacher's Guide to Endangered Peoples by Carol Malnor
(A Sharing Nature With Children Series of Teacher's Guides)
Through the activities in this Teacher's Guide, students will gain a deeper understanding and appreciation of endangered peoples of the Earth as well as their own classmates. Core curriculum objectives are met as students express and develop abilities in the multiple intelligences.

OTHER DAWN PUBLICATIONS BOOKS FOR WHICH TEACHER'S GUIDES ARE AVAILABLE

The Sharing Nature With Children Series of Teacher's Guides is distinctive in that they integrate character education with core science and language arts curricula.

Lifetimes by David Rice, introduces some of nature's longest, shortest, and most unusual lifetimes, and what they have to teach us. This book teaches, but it also goes right to the heart.

A Drop Around the World by Barbara Shaw McKinney, follows a single drop of water—from snow to steam, from polluted to purified, from stratus cloud to subterranean crack. Drop inspires our respect for water's unique role on Earth.

A Swim through the Sea by Kristin Joy Pratt, uses delightful alliterative verse and alphabet book format by this young author/illustrator to introduce the ocean habitat.

A Walk in the Rainforest by Kristin Joy Pratt, uses the original artwork and alliterative verse of this teenage author/illustrator to explore the exotic animals and plants of the tropical rainforest.

A Fly in the Sky by Kristin Joy Pratt, presents the world of insects, birds, and other animals of the air in alliterative verse and alphabet format.

DAWN PUBLICATIONS is dedicated to inspiring in children a deeper understanding and appreciation for all life on Earth. To order, or for a free copy of our catalog, please call 800-545-7475. Please also visit our web site at www.DawnPub.com.